JORDAN FIRE-FITS

Iconic Footwear

Coloring Book

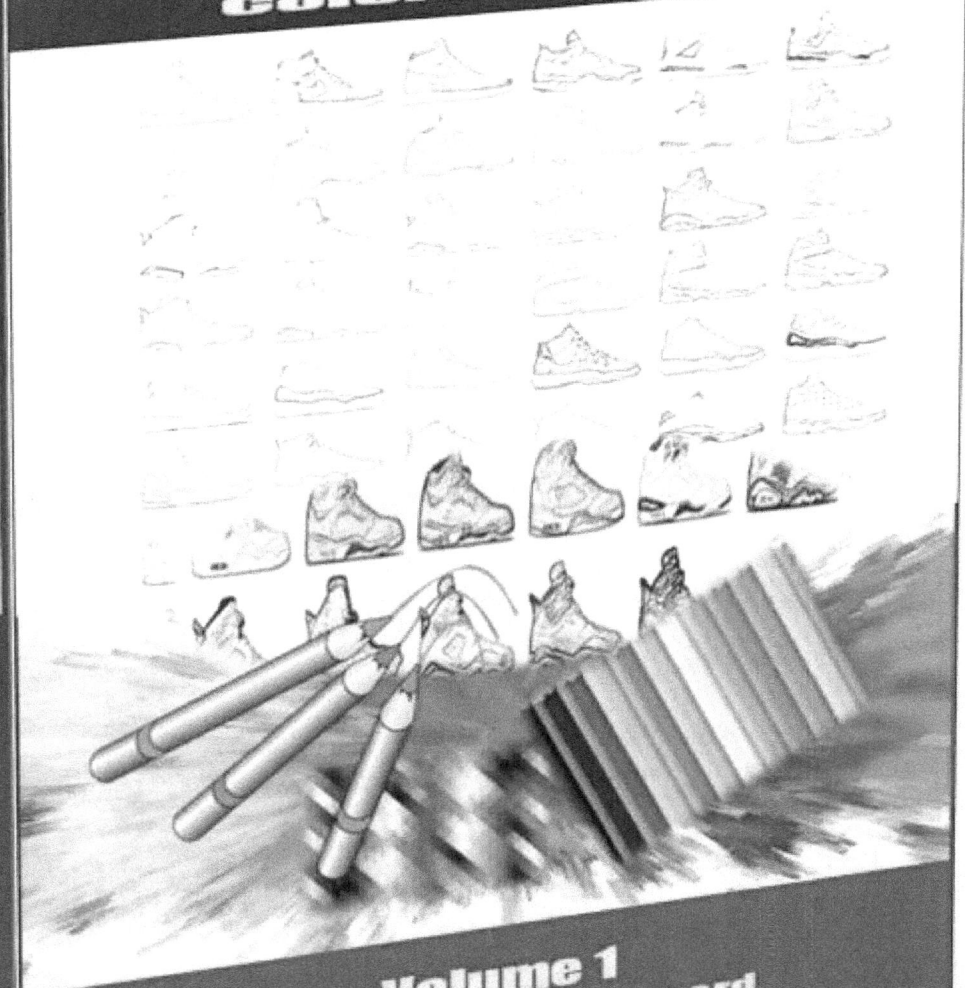

Volume 1

By Brian Ernest Hayward

JORDAN FIRE-FITS

Iconic Footwear
Coloring Book

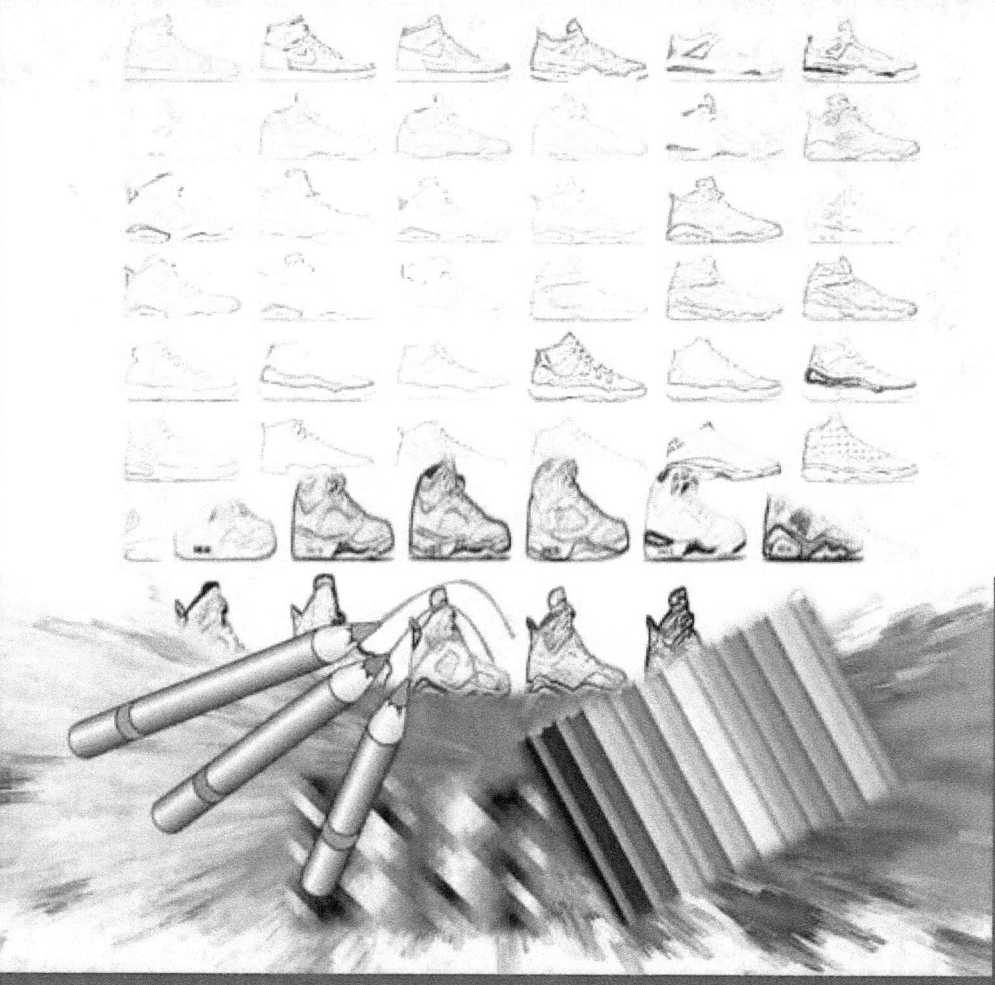

Volume 1
By Brian Ernest Hayward

Copyright © 2017 by Brian Ernest Hayward and Published by

Brian Hayward for Hayward House Publishing

Published by Hayward House and Big Book Box A Member of the Brian

Hayward Group

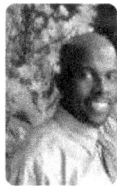

Library of Congress Cataloging-in-Publication Data

Hayward, Brian. TITLE=**HOW TO**, Journaling for success in your life / Brian Hayward. p. cm.

F.Q.T. **FREE QUICK TIPS**

ISBN-13: 978-1983430343

ISBN-10: 198343034X

Self-control. 2. Self-management (Psychology) 3. Success. 4. Success in business.

Big Book Box Press books are available at special discounts for bulk purchases

in the U.S. by corporat io ns, institut io ns, and other organizat io ns . For more

information, please contact the Special Markets Department at the Big Book Box

Books Group, 4613 Lanier drive, 4th Floor, Savannah, Ga 31405,or call (912) 224-

7502, or visit us at:

https://www.amazon.com/Brian-Ernest-Hayward/e/B06XT464NM

CHECK OUT BRIAN'S OTHER BOOKS

(his writings touch on over 400 different subjects.)

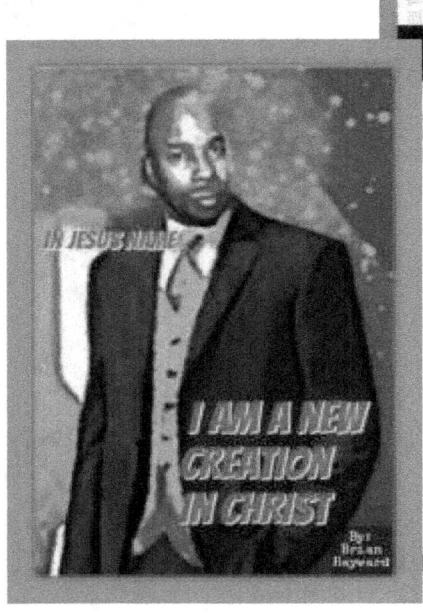
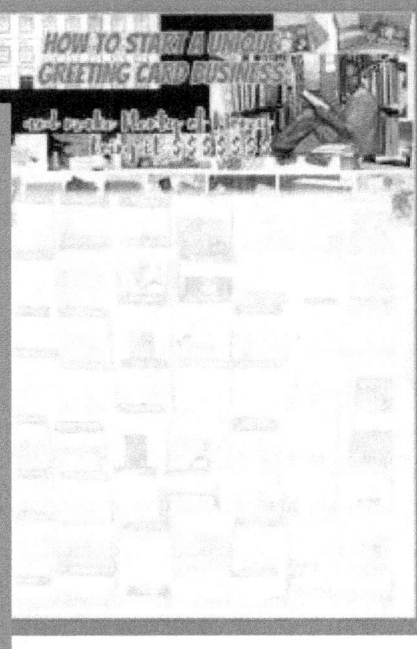
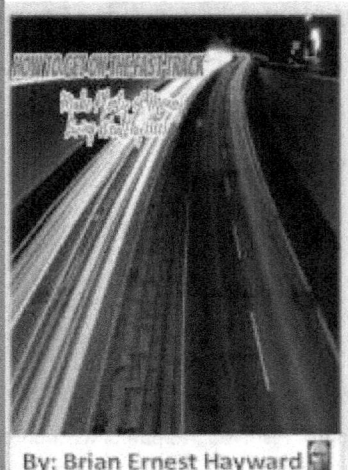

By: Brian Ernest Hayward

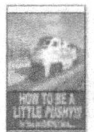
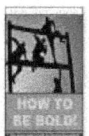
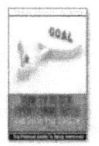
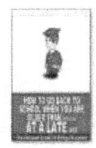
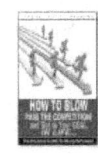

Get All Brian's Books For
Your reading pleasure Today!!

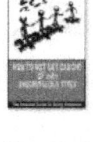
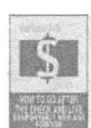
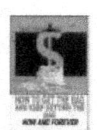
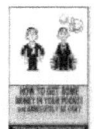
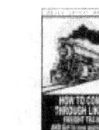
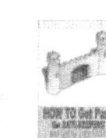
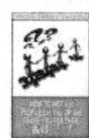
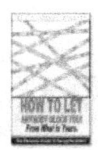
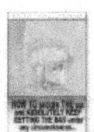

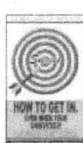

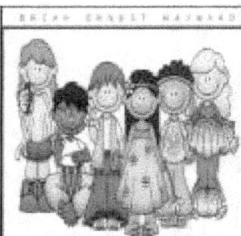
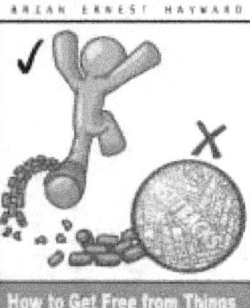
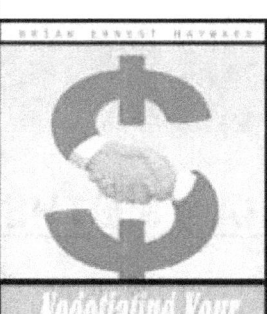
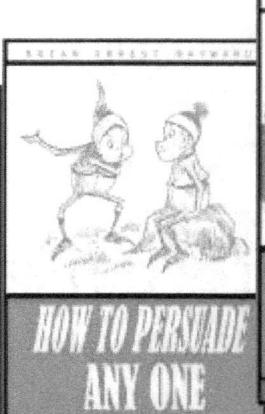
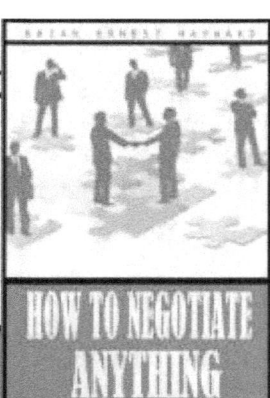

BRIAN ERNEST HAYWARD

HOW TO NOT BE Other PEOPLES FALL-GUY
under any circumstances...

The Personal Guide To Being Persistent

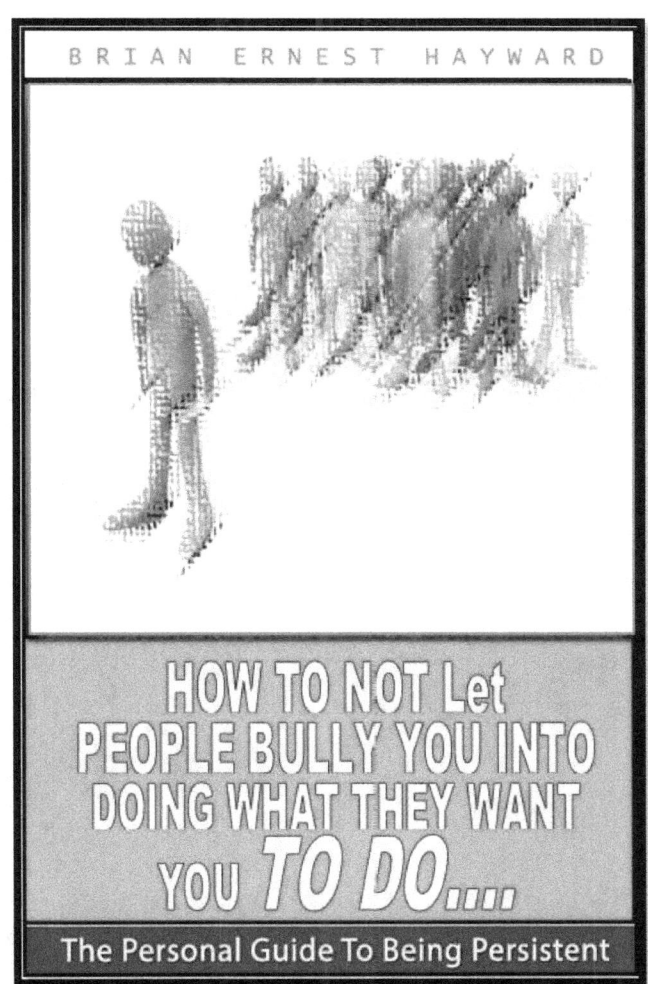

BRIAN ERNEST HAYWARD

HOW TO NOT Let PEOPLE BULLY YOU INTO DOING WHAT THEY WANT YOU *TO DO*....

The Personal Guide To Being Persistent

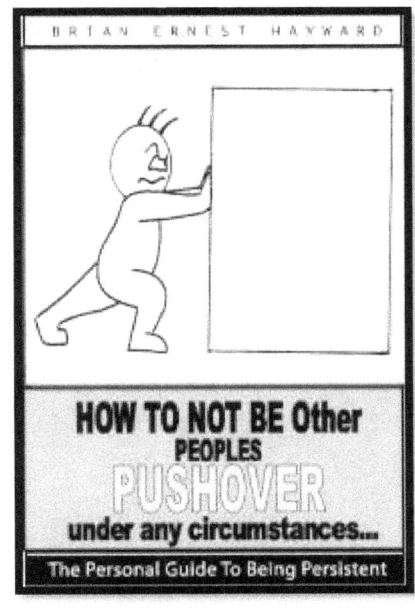

BRIAN ERNEST HAYWARD

HOW TO NOT BE Other PEOPLES PUSHOVER
under any circumstances...

The Personal Guide To Being Persistent

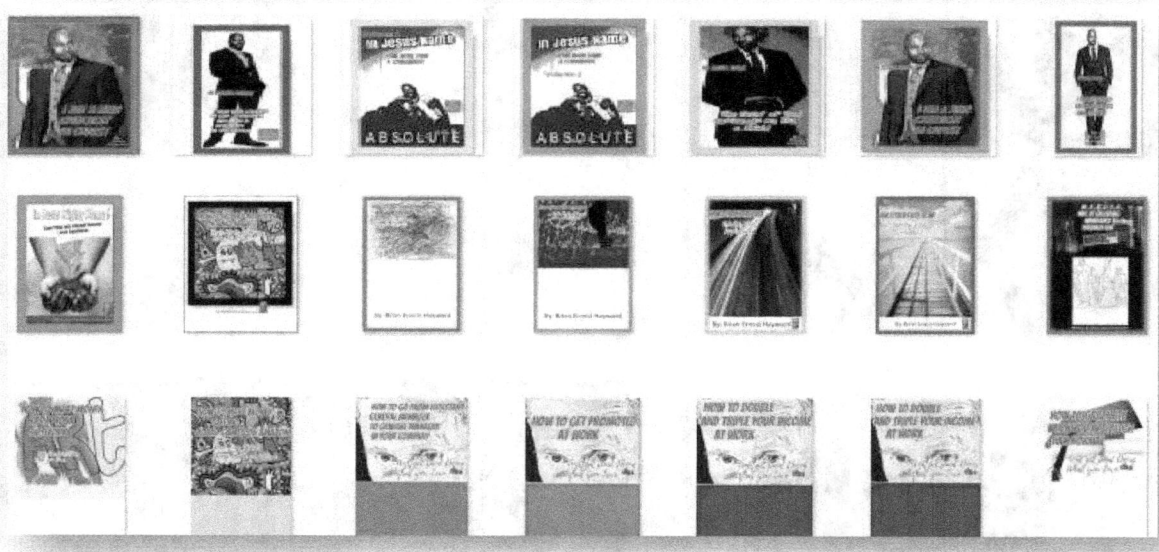

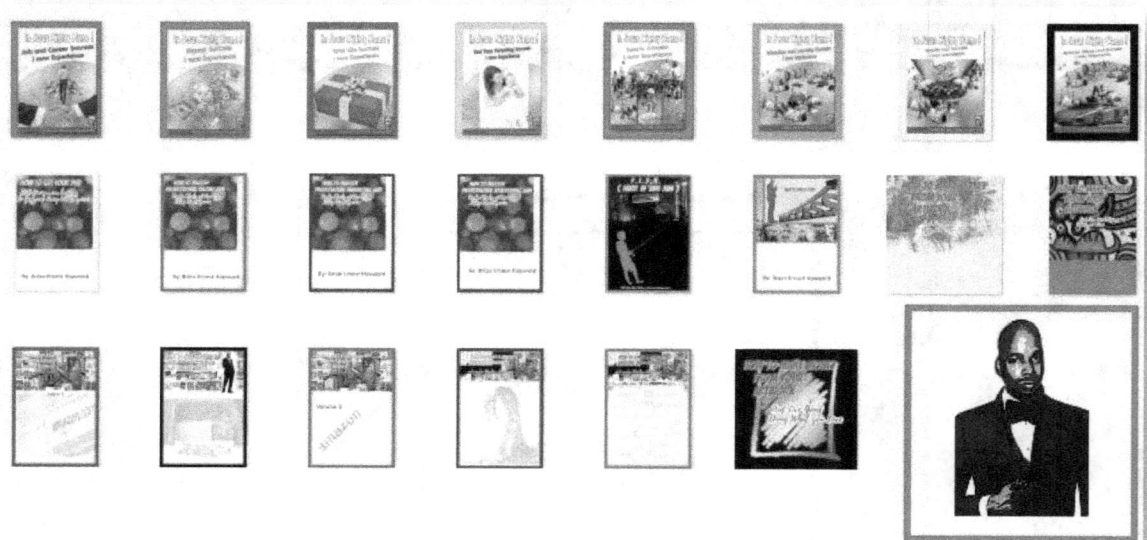

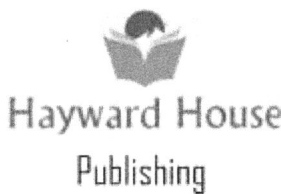

Hayward House
Publishing

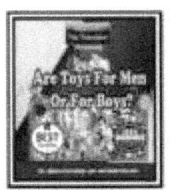
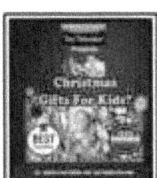
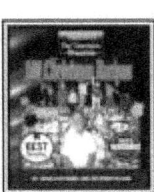
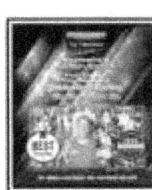
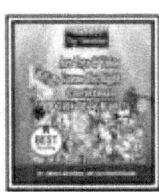
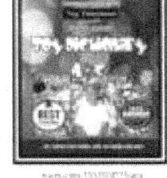

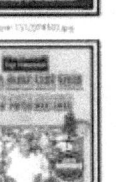
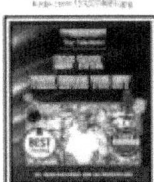
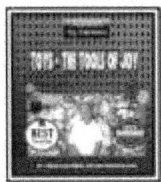
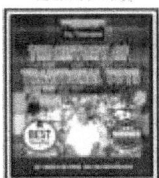

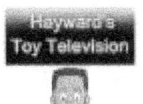
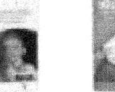
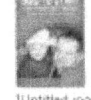
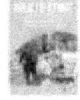
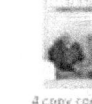
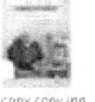
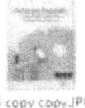
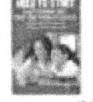

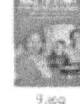

1_rex copy copy.jpg   1Untitled.jpg   3.jpg   4 copy copy.jpg   5 copy copy.JPG   6 copy copy.JPG   7 copy copy.jpg   8.jpg   9.jpg

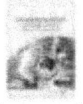
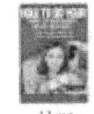
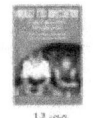
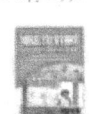
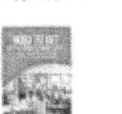

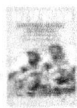

10 copy copy.jpg   11 copy copy.JPG   12 copy copy.JPG   13.jpg   14.jpg   15 copy copy.jpg   16 copy copy.jpg   17 copy copy.jpg   18.jpg   19.jpg

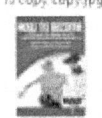
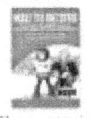
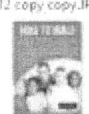

20 copy copy.jpg   21 copy copy.jpg   22.jpg   23 copy copy.jpg

Get The Whole Series

AUTHOR BIOGRAPHY

Brian Ernest Hayward is a passionate Author and Inspirational Speaker, internationally known for his unwavering dedication to creating positive change through the power of words. From religious and success books, to adult coloring books and artist how-tos, his writings touch on over 400 different subjects.

Today, all of Brian's publications are sold worldwide across multiple formats (Paperback, Kindle, and Large Print) and are translated into 21 different languages. He has also participated in over 100 speaking engagements spanning over 38 states.

INTRODUCTION

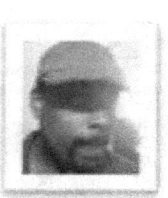 *I was taught by my teacher, Pastor Bill Winston, this prayer. This prayer has served me well, and in due time it will serve you well. Father I come before you in Jesus name, thank you for the anointing that's on me and these lips of clay. I know that because of your blessing, I speak this word today with excellency, accuracy, and boldness.*

I thank you for thinking through my mind and speaking through my lips and this word will come forth unhindered, and unchecked by any outside force. Now I give you the praise for it and I fully expect signs, wonders, and miracles to confirm your word preached in Jesus name, Amen! This is a book about the "new creation" God has made me through Christ Jesus. Be inspired as you read toward greatness and achievement.

YOUR PORTION

Another of My teachers is Pastor Dr. Uebert Angel. Dr Uebert Angel is a very good bible teacher. Check out his books very soon, if you have not already. He mentioned this verse in his book entitled: God's Get Rich Quick Scheme. He notes, "Thus saith the LORD, thy Redeemer, the Holy One of Israel; I am the LORD thy God which teacheth thee to profit, which leadeth thee by the way that thou shouldest go. Isaiah 48:17 Do you see that, he teaches you to profit, by his word, by his spiritual laws, he wants to lead you the way you should go and that way is not into a financial wilderness, it's to take you to a place of the overflow for Jesus came so that you should have life and have it abundantly.

Lack is not your portion, sickness is not your portion, poverty is not your portion, and generational curses are not your portion. Work towards a seed, find good ground, sow your seed and act upon what you have sowed for, you will surely come back with a testimony.

MAKE THIS CONFESSION BEFORE READING THIS BOOK

MAKE THIS FULL CONFESSION EACH NIGHT FOR THE NEXT 30 DAYS. "I am a winner. I am blessed coming by in and blessed going out. I am blessed in all my efforts. I am blessed in all my undertakings. I am blessed even when I merely try. God's grace gives me greater victories even when I start later than others. Everything I put my hands to is blessed. Everything I show interest in acquiring, I am blessed with achieving. My mind is blessed in everything I think of. My ideas are blessed. My ideas are blessed with heavenly creativity. God prepared my deliverance before the foundation of the earth and he has already made all crooked places straight and opened doors that men have said are impossible to open. I am blessed with God's word

I keep sound wisdom and discretion. Wisdom resides in my heart and knowledge is pleasant to my soul. Discretion preserves me. Understanding keeps me and delivers me from all evil. My ways are ways of pleasantness and all my paths are peace. Thank You, Father, I always find wisdom for she says, "I love them that love me; And those that seek me early shall find me." I trust in the Lord with all my heart, and lean not to my own understanding.

I am born of incorruptible seed; And I walk and live by faith. Wisdom leads me when I go; keeps me when I sleep, and speaks with me when I wake. I refuse to accept any lies from the devil. The Holy Spirit is my Teacher, and guides me into all truth.

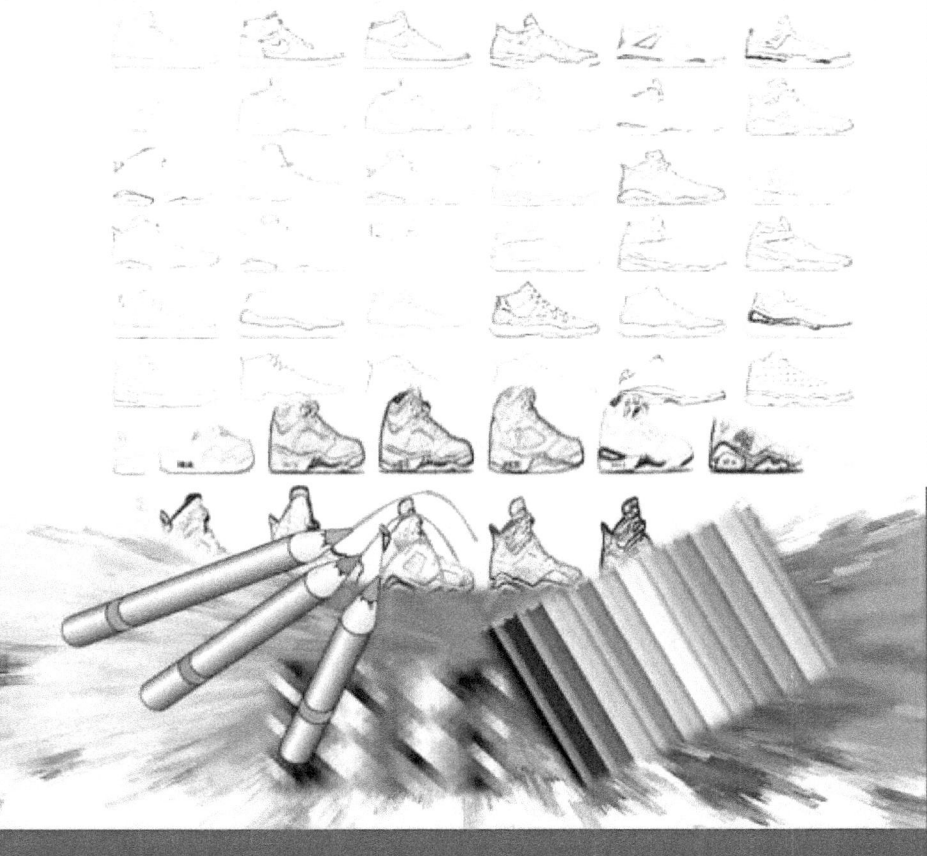

JORDAN FIRE-FITS

Iconic Footwear
Coloring Book

Volume 1
By Brian Ernest Hayward

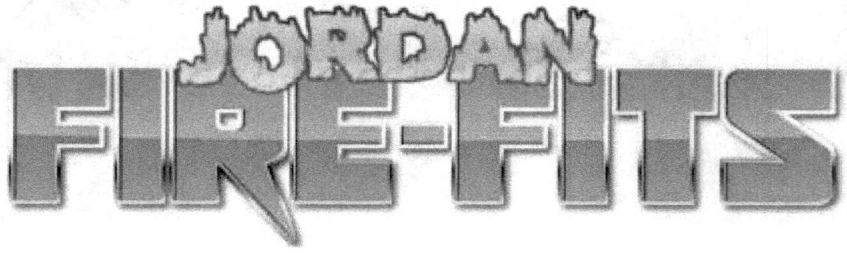

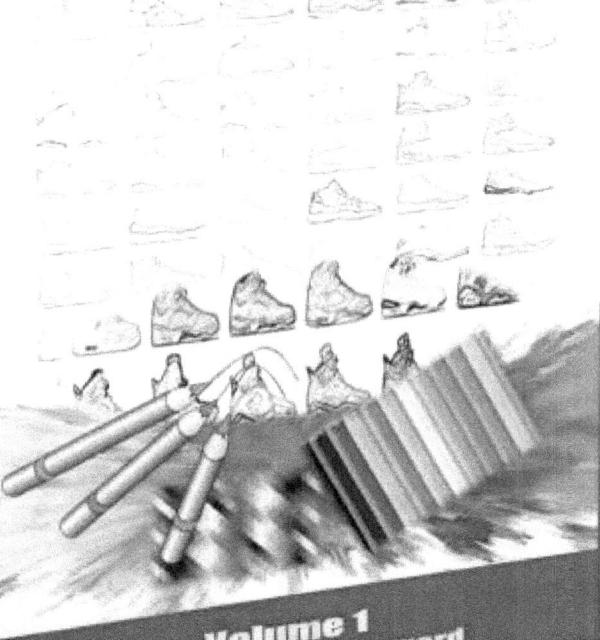

JORDAN FIRE-FITS

Iconic Footwear
Coloring Book

Volume 1
By Brian Ernest Hayward

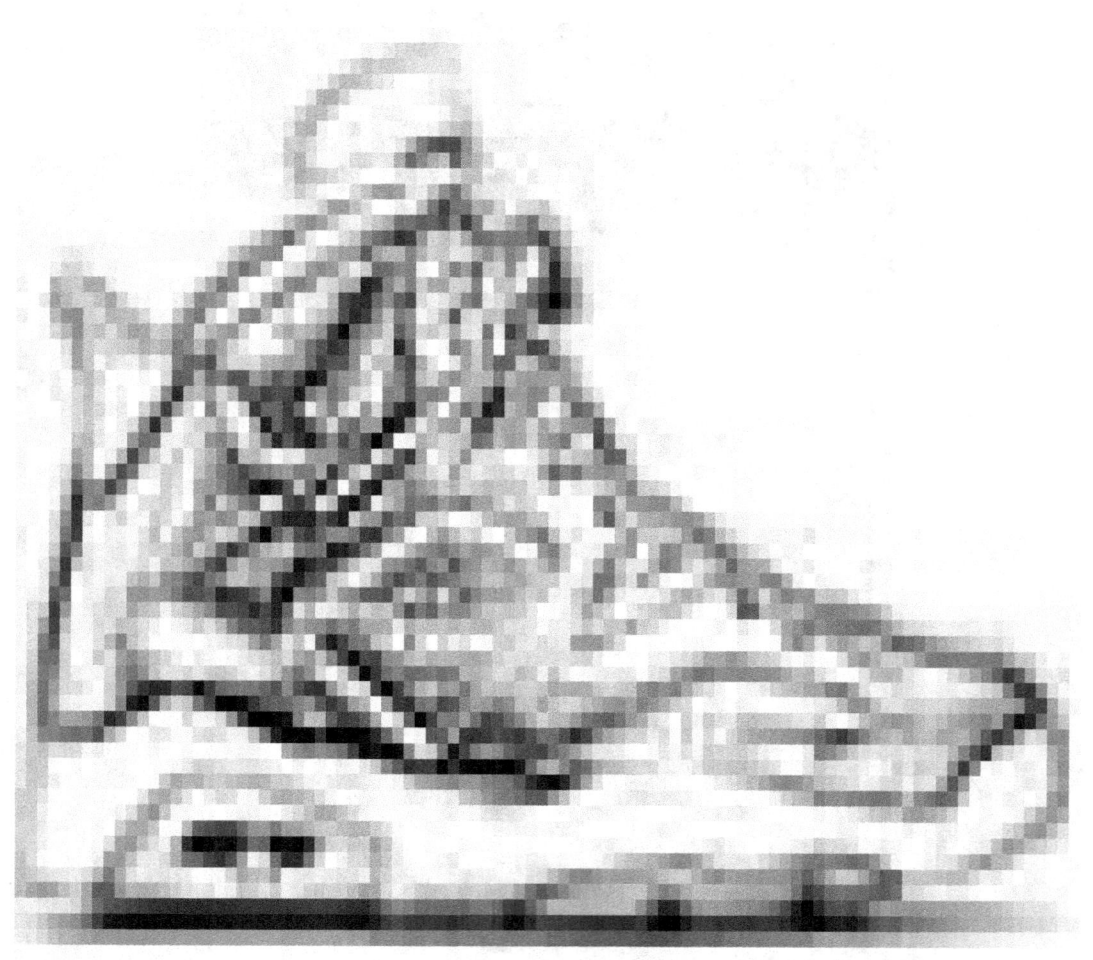

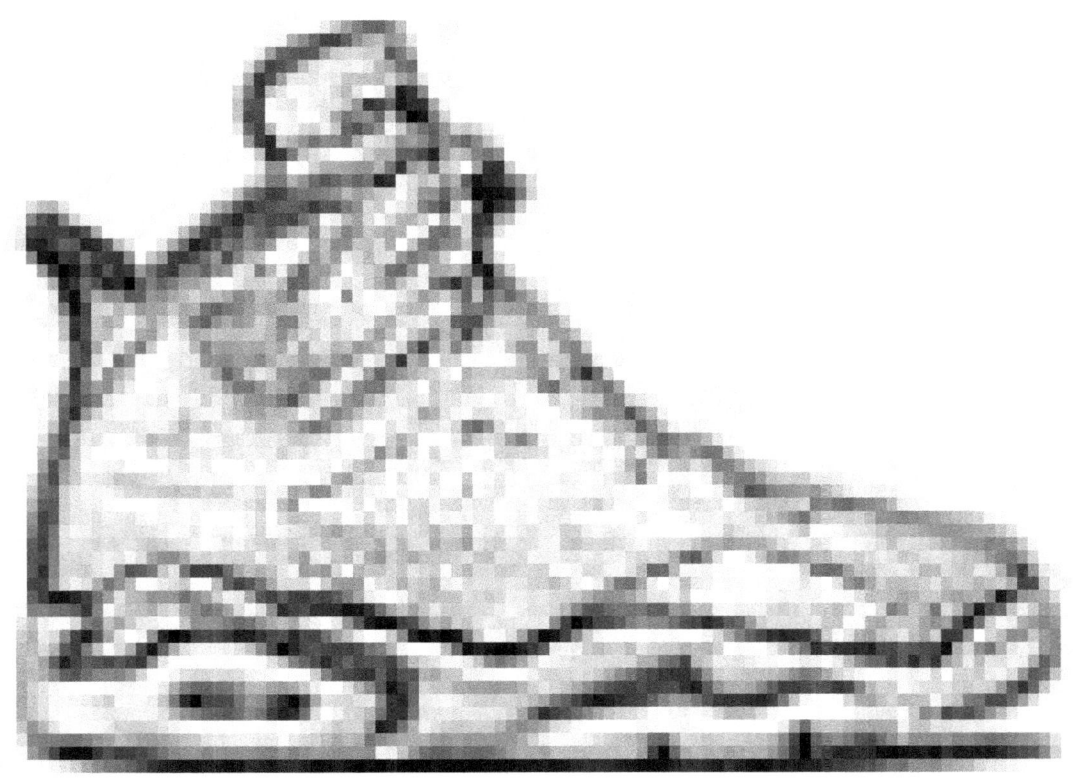

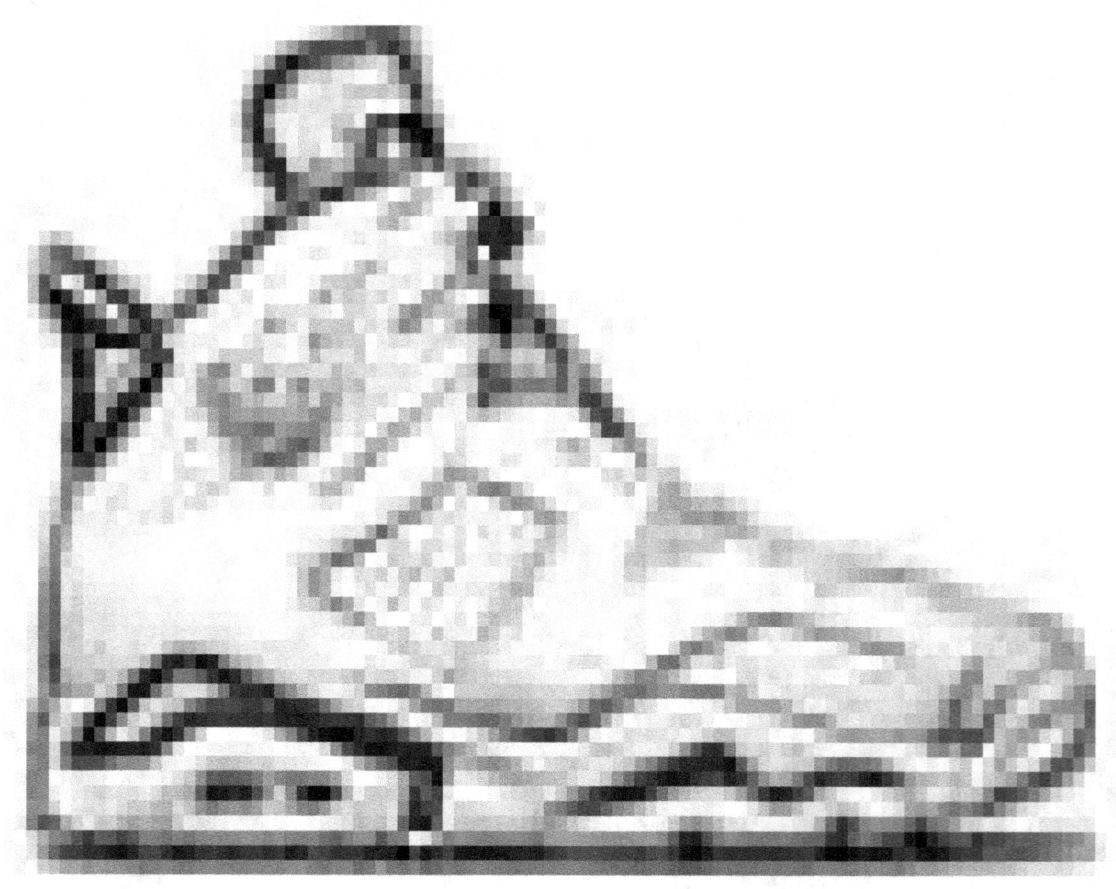

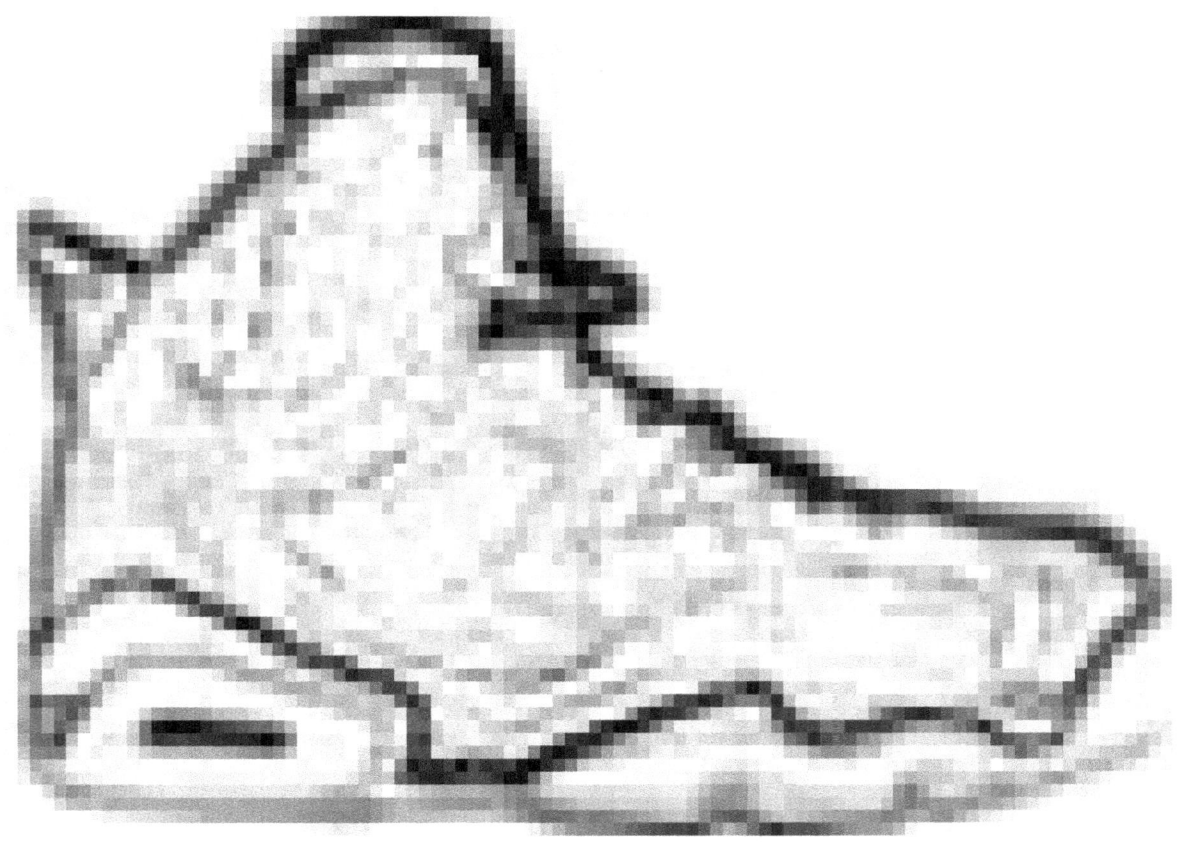

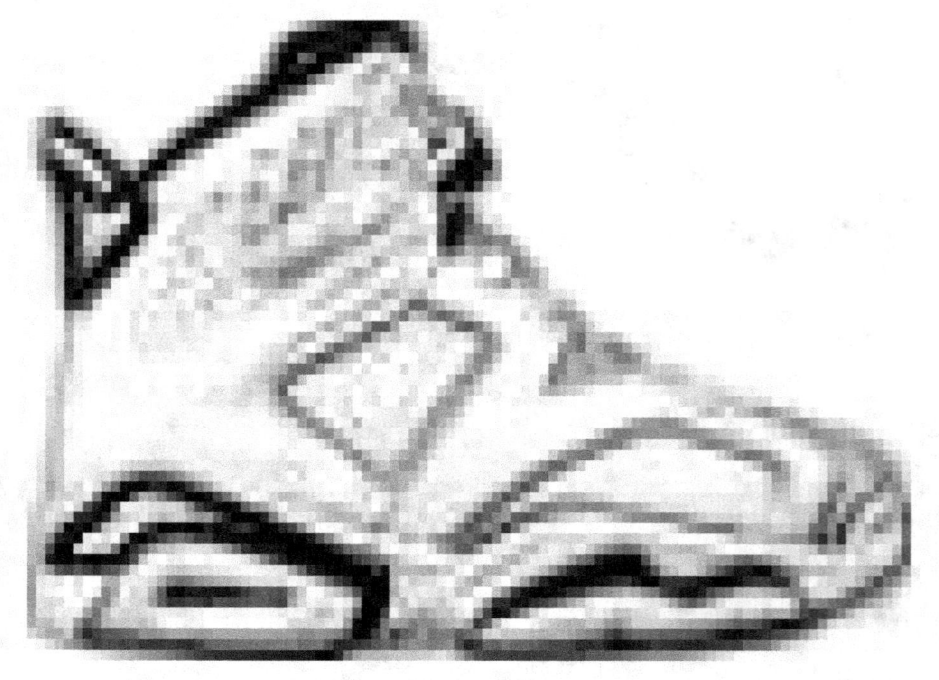

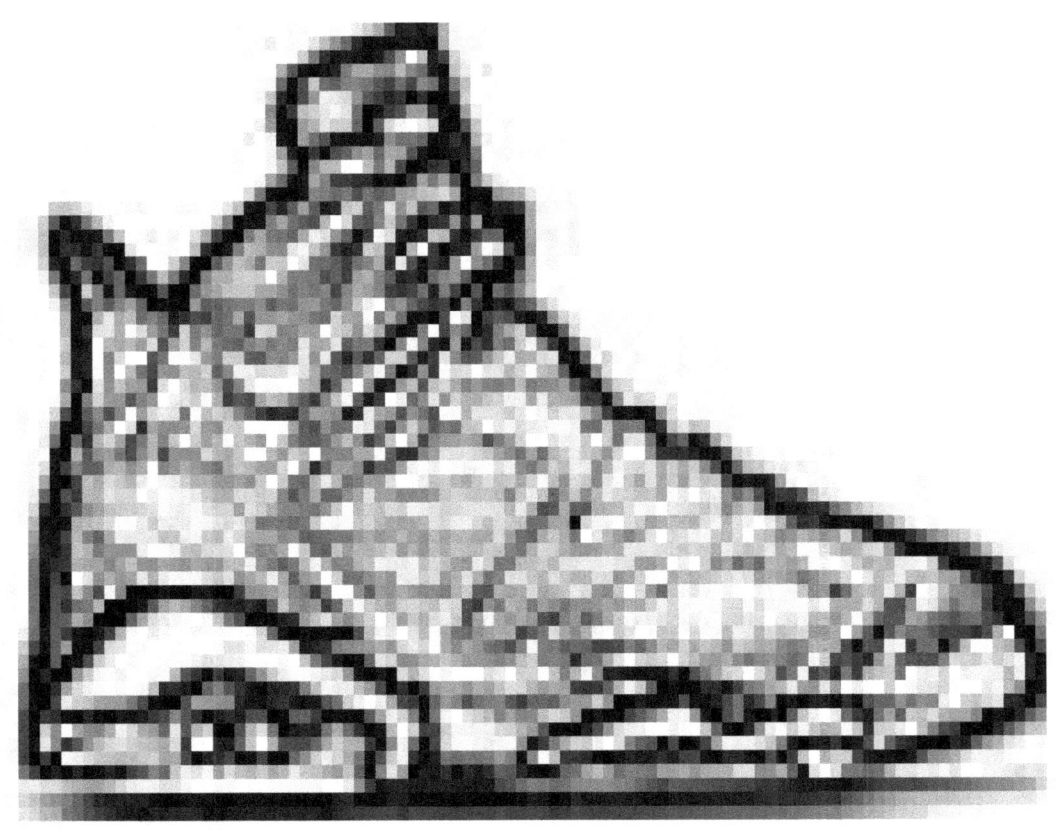

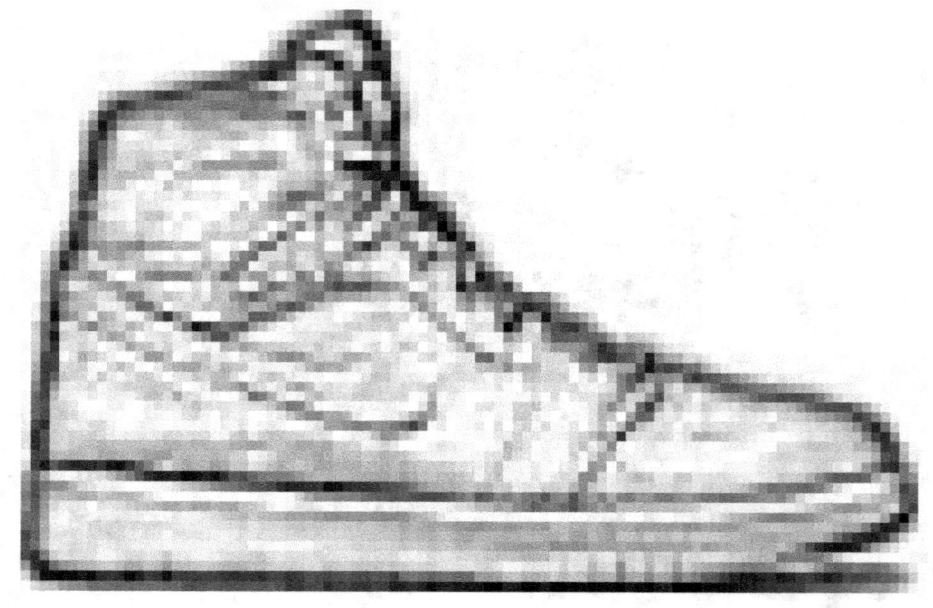

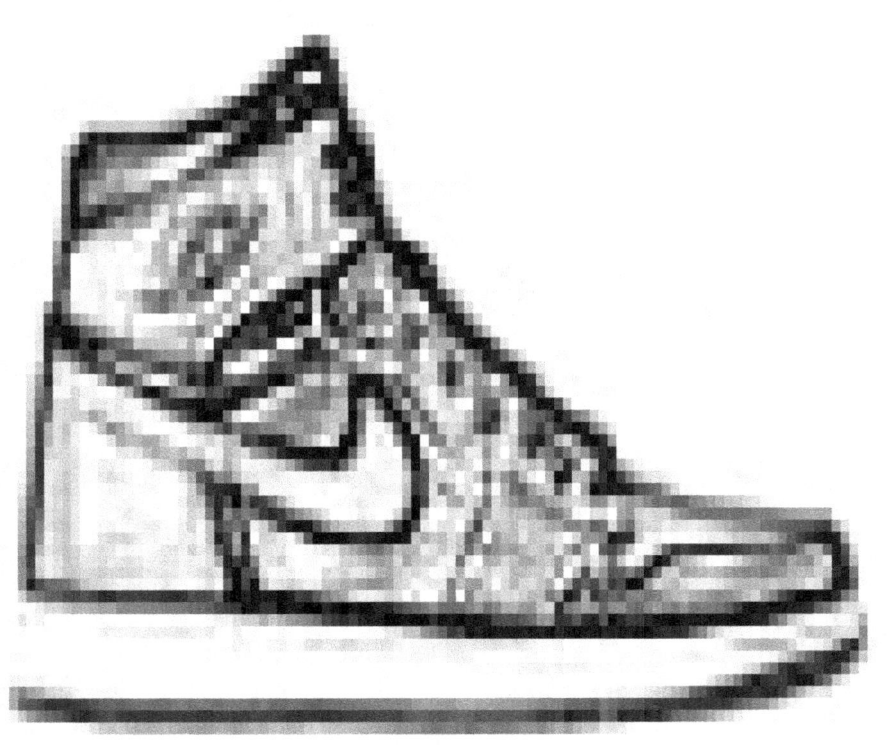

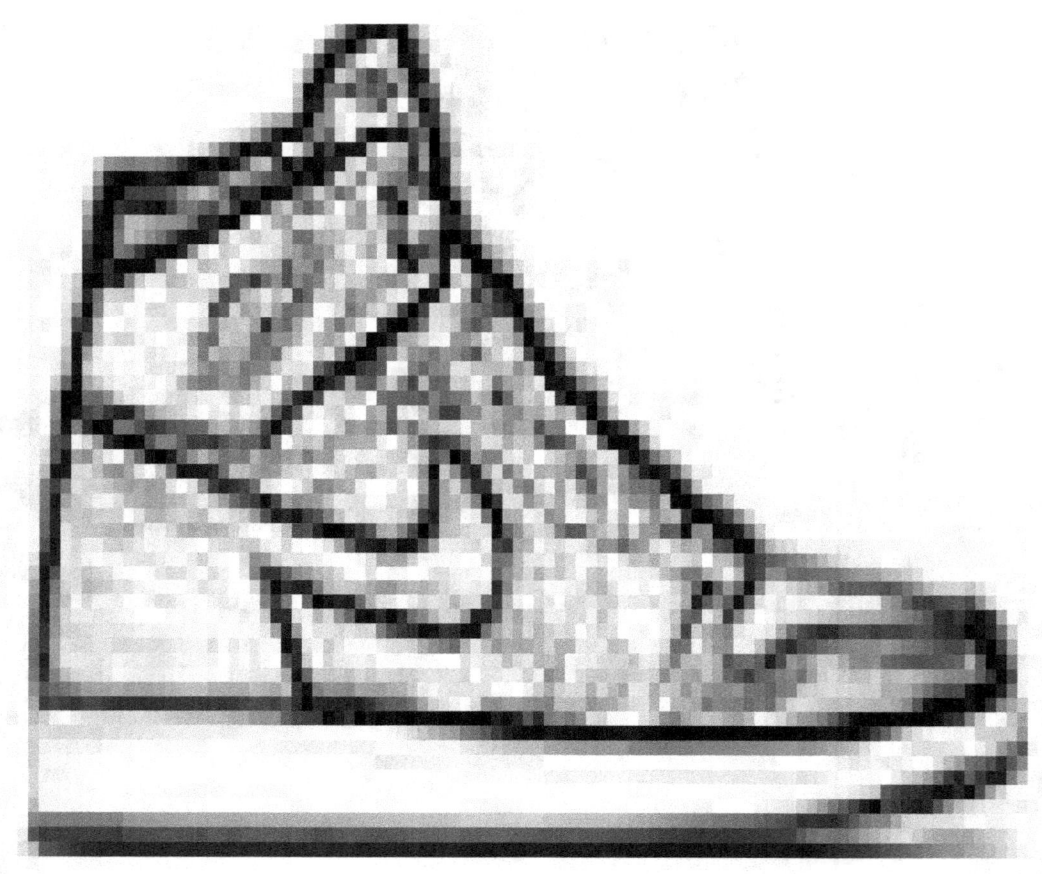

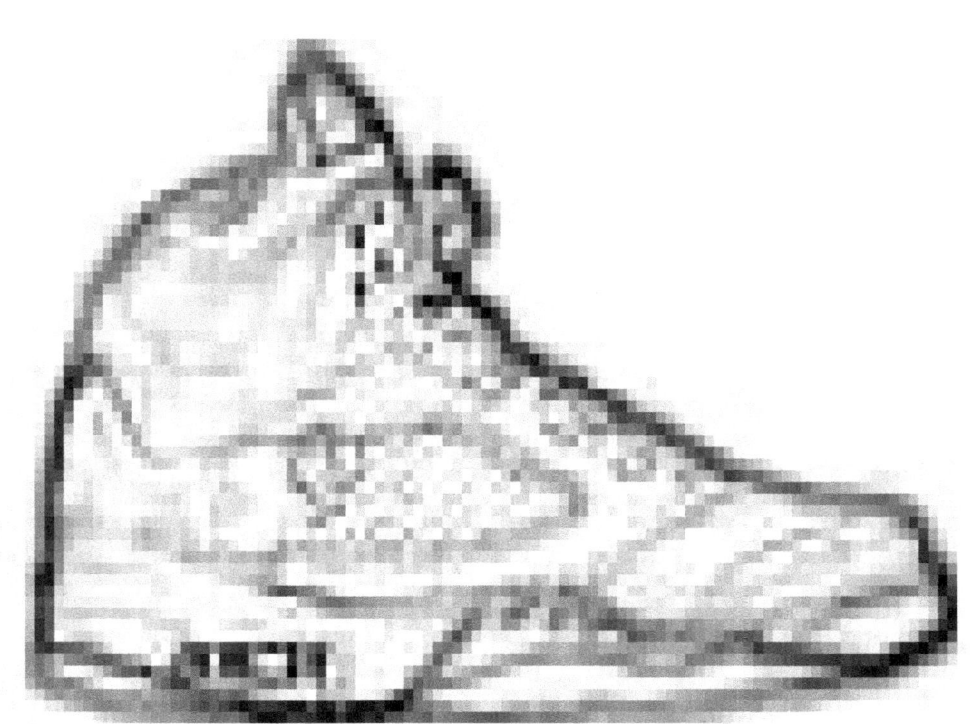

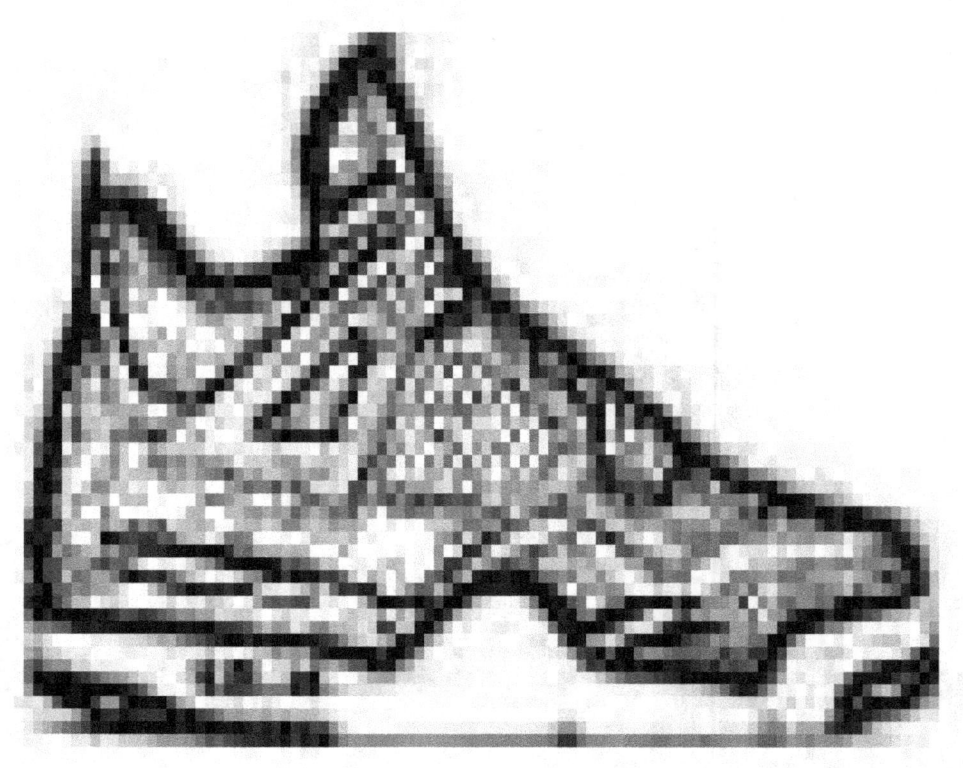

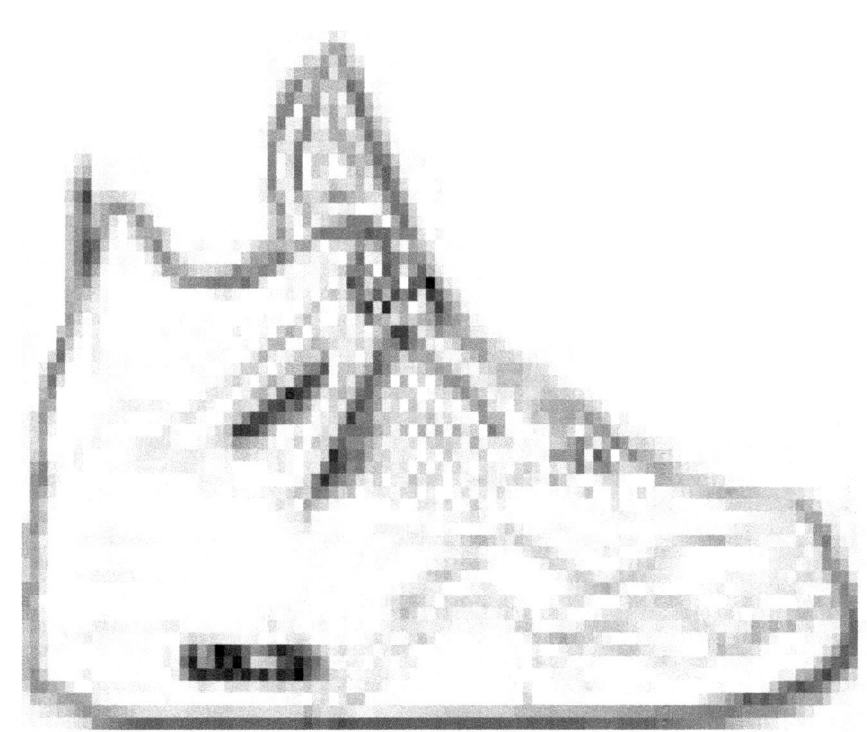

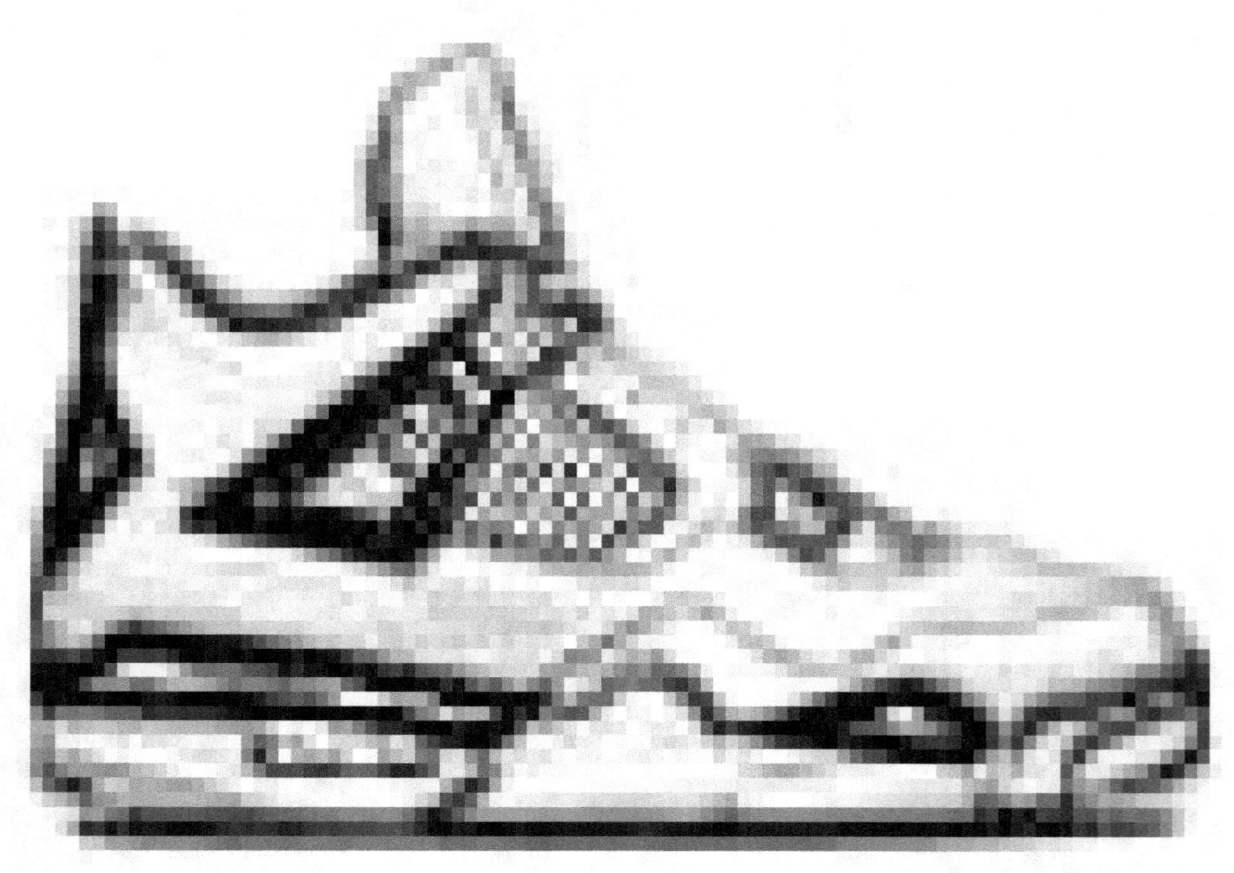

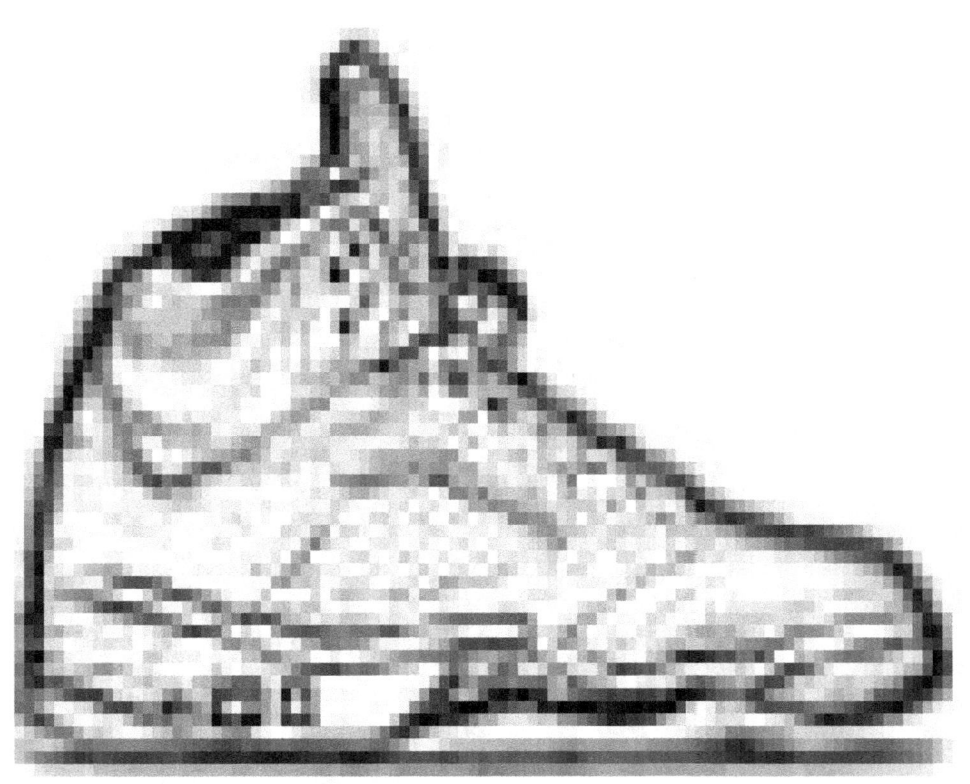

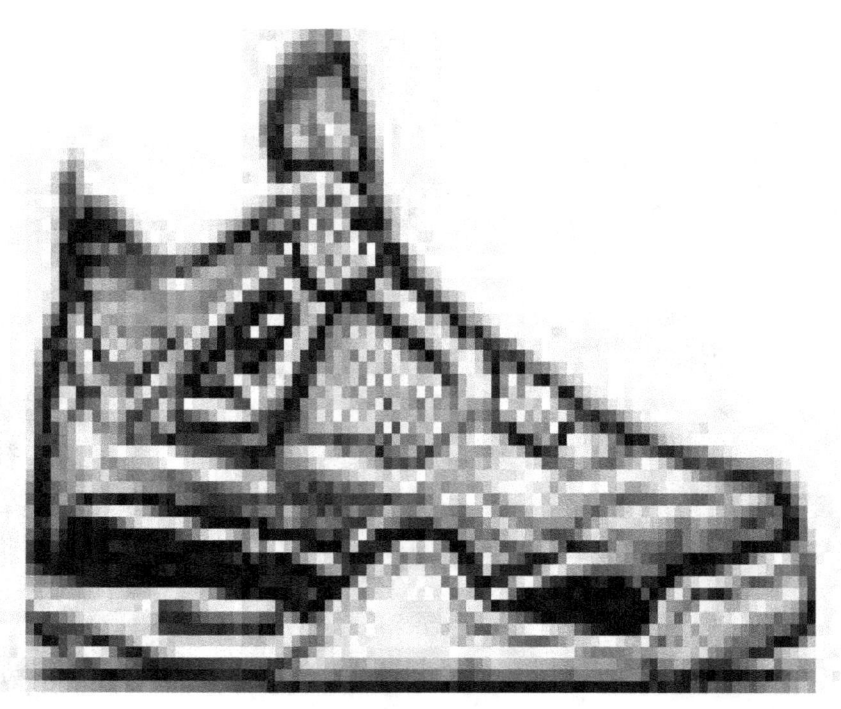

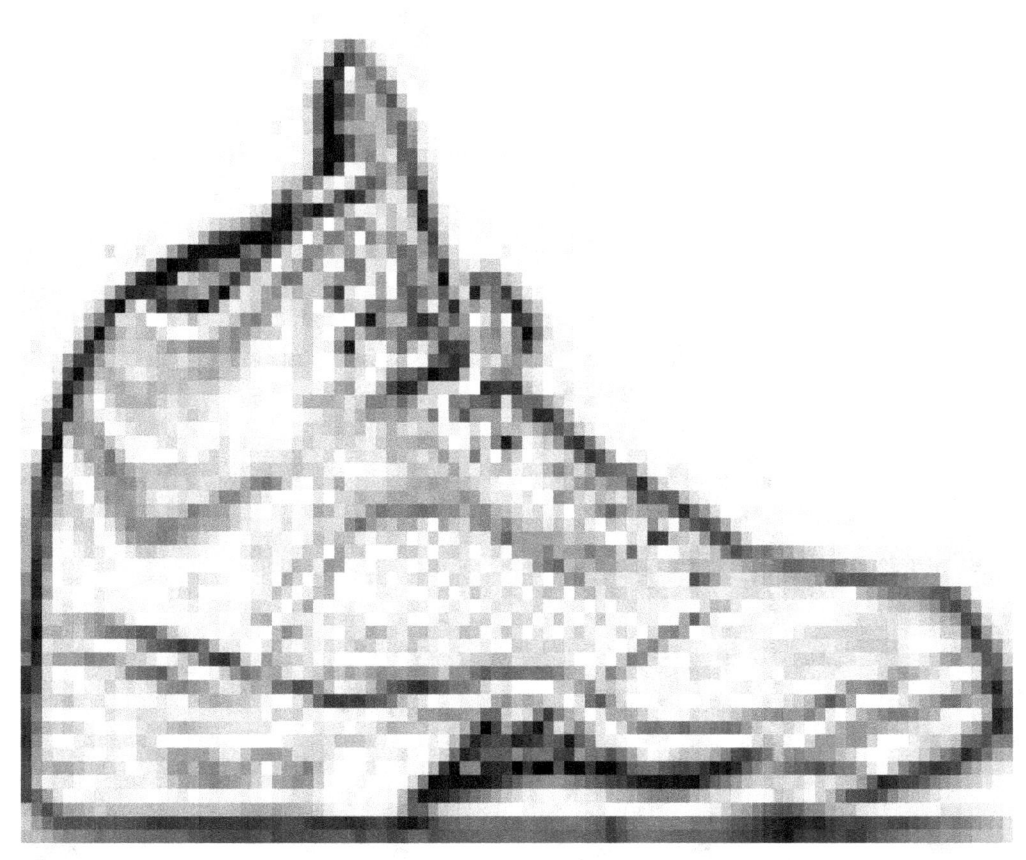

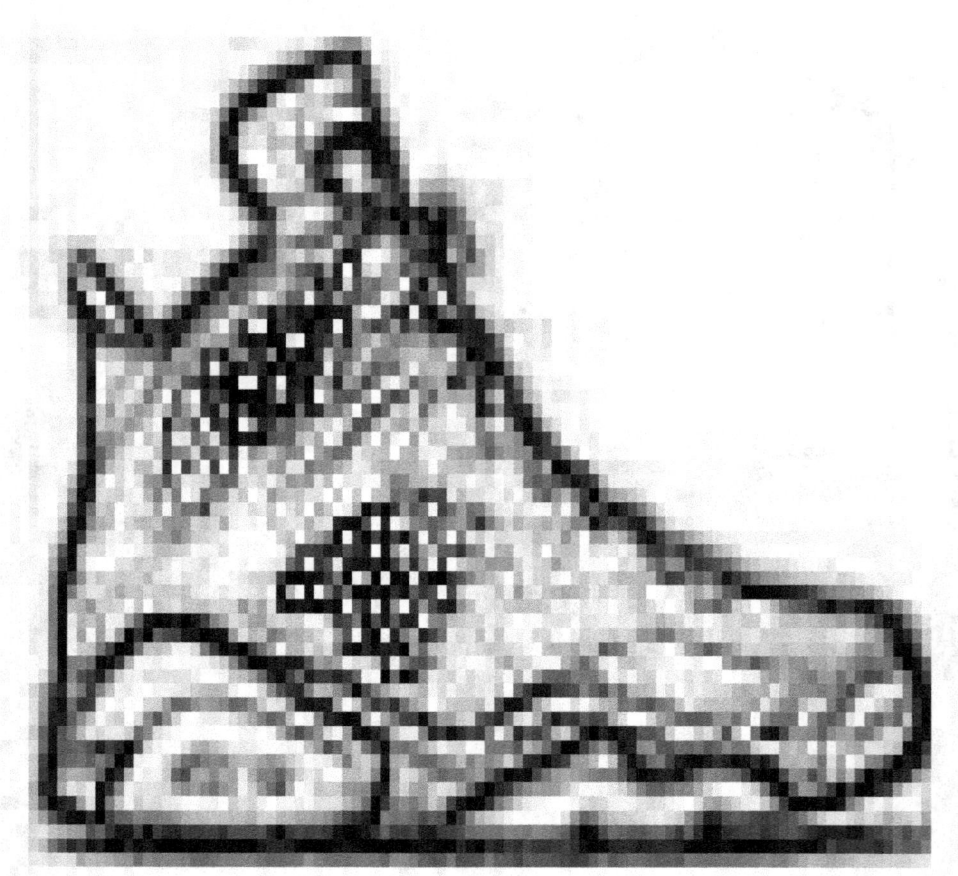

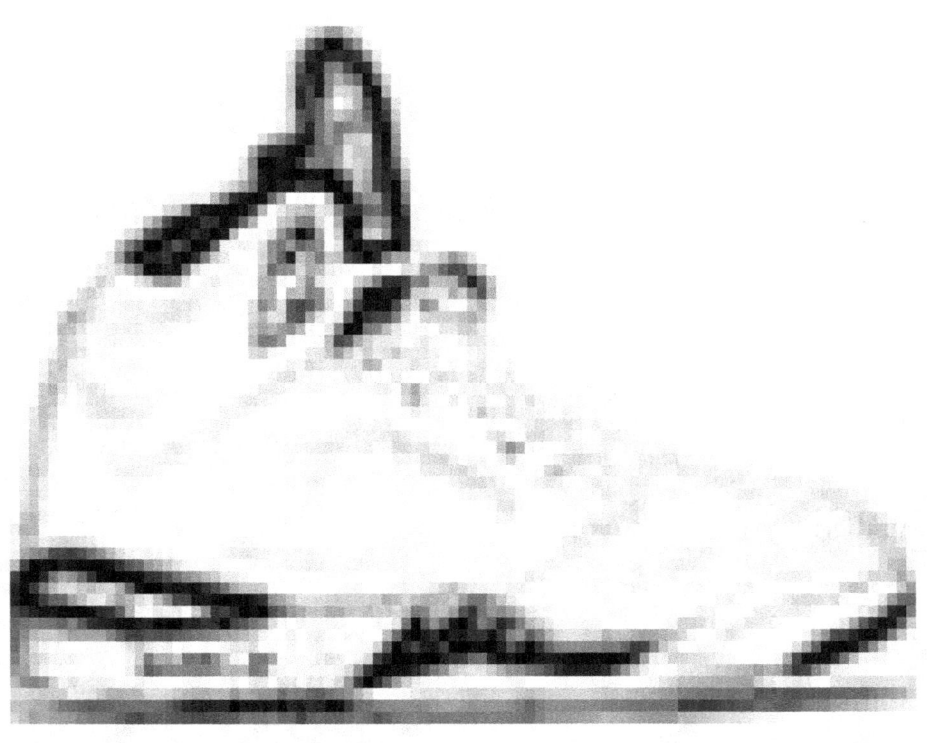

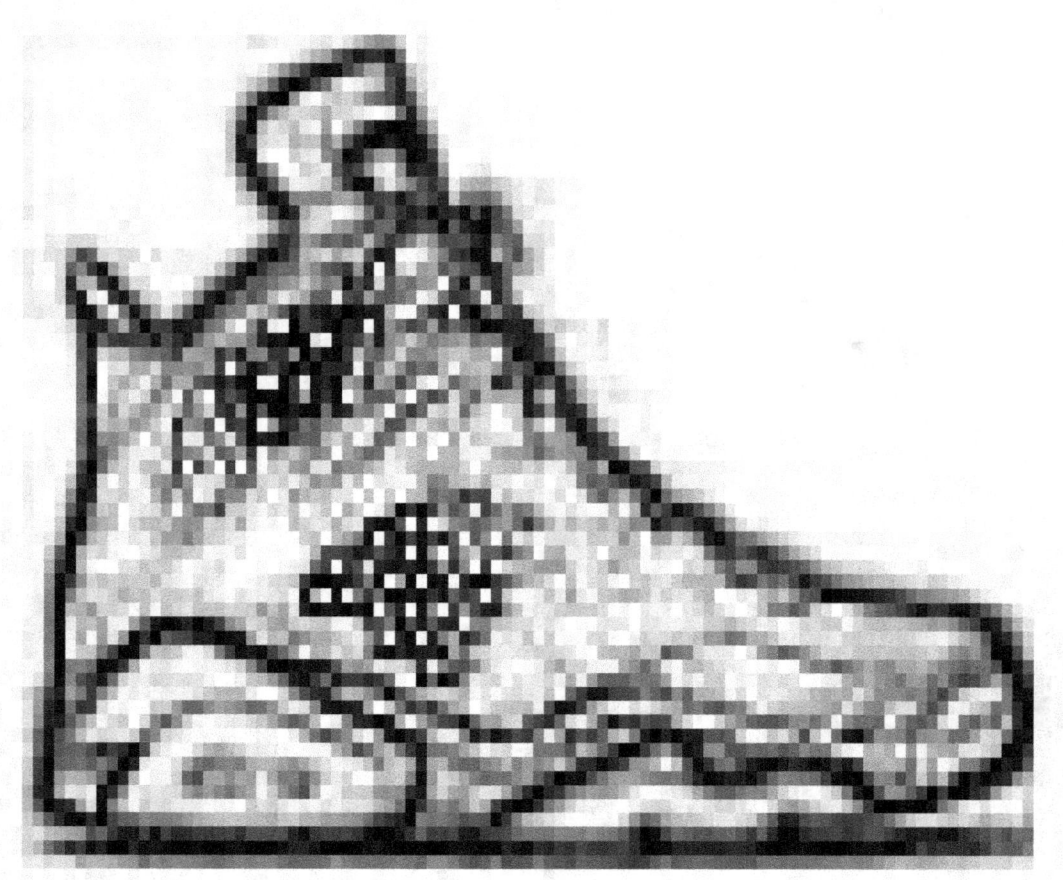

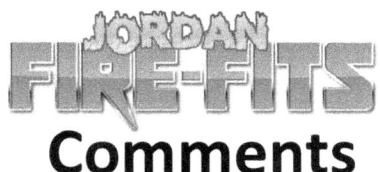

Comments

- I can't believe nobody is commenting on this. Jordon 7 Bordeaux is the best of all time. They left them out. Jordan 6 in black and red is second place.
- Wow i never knew there were more than 15 Jordan's
- Jordan, He wore the 9s in the space jam movie so technically he did wear them
- My favorites is 1,3,4,5,11,12,13 my favorite one out of all is the 12s
- You guys need to do an updated video with the new Jordans, overall great video tho
- Idk I kinda like the gamma blue 11s more than the space jams

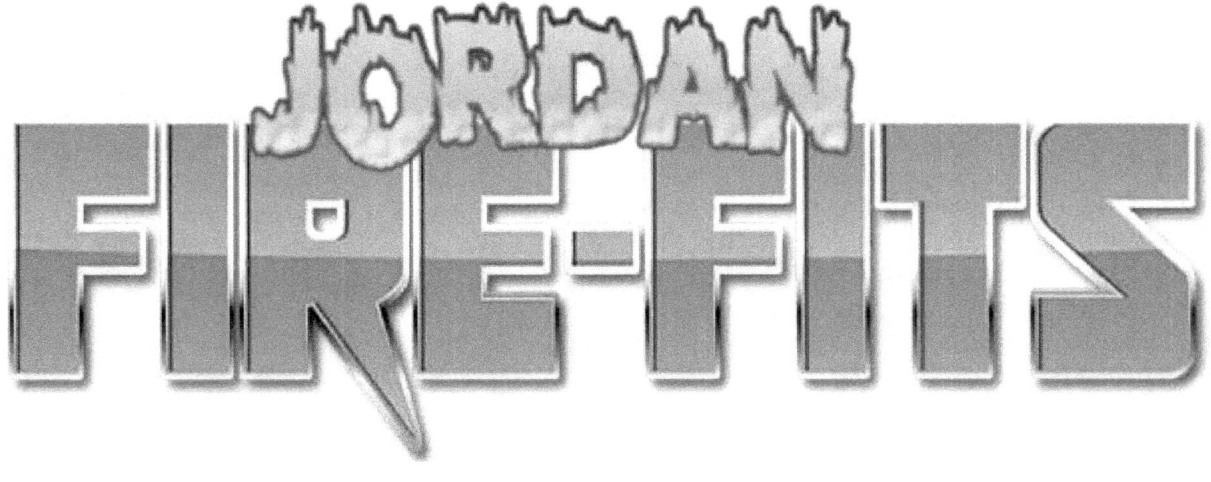

Call to Worship

Accept Jesus Today, there is No other Way!

Our Call to Worship is from John 13:34-35, the words of Jesus:
"I give you a new commandment, that you love one another.
Just as I have loved you, you also should love one another.
By this everyone will know that you are my disciples,
if you have love for one another."
Let's pray:
Loving God,
we come to worship today because we love you,
and we want to love you more.
We come to worship needing love in our lives:
love for family, friends, strangers, enemies.
In this hour of worship,
touch our hearts,
fill our hearts,
open our hearts
to your love which passes all understanding. Amen.

CHECK OUT BRIAN'S OTHER BOOKS

(his writings touch on over 400 different subjects.)

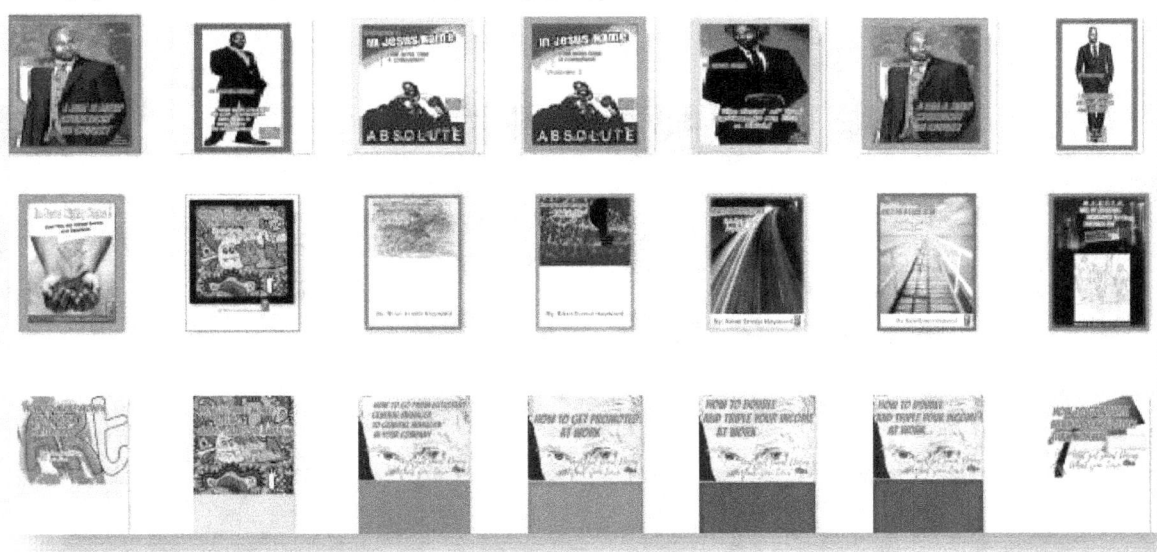

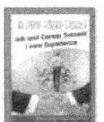 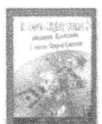 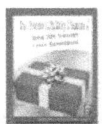 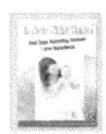 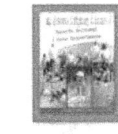 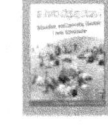 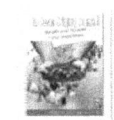 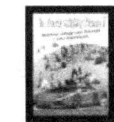

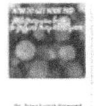 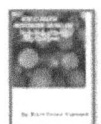 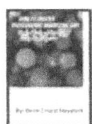 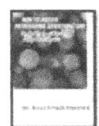 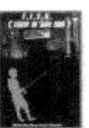 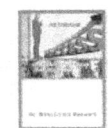 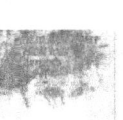 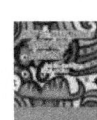

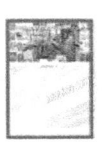 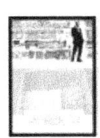 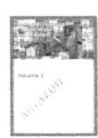 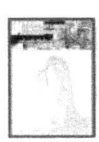 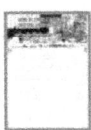 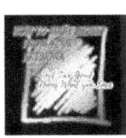 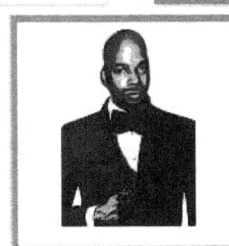

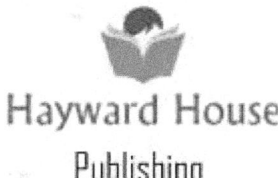

Hayward House
Publishing

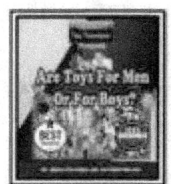 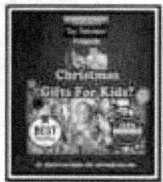 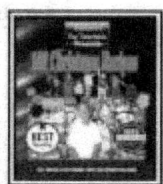 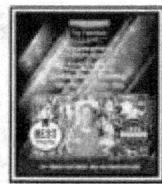 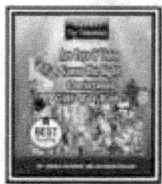 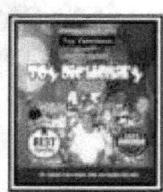

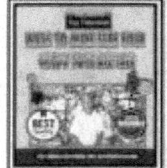 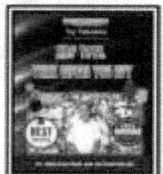 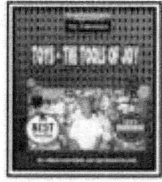 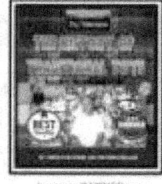 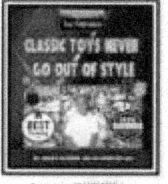

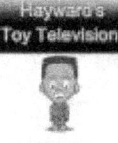

1_rev copy copy.jpg   1Untitled.jpg   3.jpg   4 copy copy.jpg   5 copy copy.JPG   6 copy copy.JPG   7 copy copy.jpg   8.jpg   9.jpg

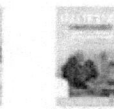  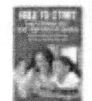 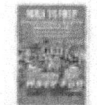 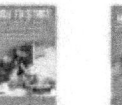

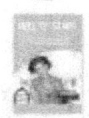 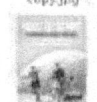 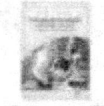  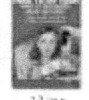   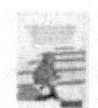 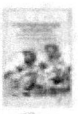

10 copy copy.jpg   11 copy copy.JPG   12 copy copy.JPG   13.jpg   14.jpg   15 copy copy.jpg   16 copy copy.jpg   17 copy copy.jpg   18.jpg   19.jpg

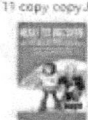  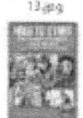

20 copy copy.jpg   21 copy copy.jpg   22.jpg   23 copy copy.jpg

Get The Whole Series

Works Cited

Berchie, Daniel. *Bible*. Cambridge Scholars Publishing, 2016.

Copeland, Kenneth. *Our Covenant with God*. Harrison House, 1999.

Copeland, Kenneth, and Gloria Copeland. *From Faith to Faith: Devotional : a Daily Guide to Victory*.

    Harrison House, 1999.

---. *Pursuit of His Presence: Daily Devotions to Strengthen Your Walk with God*. Kenneth Copeland

    Publications, 2012.

"Course Textbooks | W. W. Norton & Company." *Home | W. W. Norton & Company*,

    books.wwnorton.com/books/college-subject.aspx?id=4294983309.

The King James Study Bible: King James Version. Thomas Nelson Publishers, 2003.

Washington, Booker T, and William L. Andrews. *Up from Slavery: Authoritative Text, Contexts, and*

    Composition History, Criticism. Norton, 1996.

Winston, Bill. *Faith & the Marketplace*. 2016.

---. *The Kingdom of God in You: Discover the Greatness of God's Power Within*. Harrison House, 2010.

---. *The Law of Confession: Revolutionize Your Life and Rewrite Your Future with the Power of Words*.

    Harrison House, 2009.

---. *Training for Reigning: Releasing the Power of Your Potential*. HigherLife Development

    Services, 2011.

---. *Transform Your Thinking, Transform Your Life: Radically Change Your Thoughts, Your World, and*

    Your Destiny. Harrison House, 2008.

World's Concordance to the Holy Bible: King James Version. World Pub. Co, 1969.

https://www.biblegateway.com/quicksearch/?quicksearch=jehovah&qs_version=KJV

http://biblehub.com/mark/4-38.htm

http://biblereasons.com/fishing/

https://www.google.com/search?q=all+equipment+needed+to+fish&ie=utf-8&oe=utf-8&aq=t&q=all+equipment+needed+to+fish&ie=utf-8&oe=utf-8&aq=t&channel=fflb&q=all+equipment+needed+to+fish&ie=utf-8&oe=utf-8&aq=t&channel=rcs

http://www.knowyourphrase.com/phrase-meanings/Give-a-Man-a-Fish.html

http://www.christianbiblereference.org/faq_faith.htm

https://bible.knowing-jesus.com/words/Fish-hook

https://bible.knowing-jesus.com/topics/Fishes

https://www.allaboutgod.com/jesus-fish.htm

http://biblehub.com/matthew/4-4.htm

http://www.biblemeanings.info/Words/Animal/Fishes.htm

http://www.patheos.com/blogs/christiancrier/2015/07/17/what-does-water-represent-in-the-bible-a-christian-study/

https://www.copyscape.com/prosearch.php

https://www.biblegateway.com/quicksearch/?quicksearch=jehovah&qs_version=KJV

http://biblehub.com/mark/4-38.htm

http://biblereasons.com/fishing/

http://www.knowyourphrase.com/phrase-meanings/Give-a-Man-a-Fish.html

http://www.christianbiblereference.org/faq_faith.htm

https://bible.knowing-jesus.com/words/Fish-hook

https://bible.knowing-jesus.com/topics/Fishes

https://www.google.com/search?q=faith+confessions+about+faith&ie=utf-8&oe=utf-8&aq=t&q=faith+confessions+about+faith&ie=utf-8&oe=utf-8&aq=t&channel=fflb&q=faith+confessions+about+faith&ie=utf-8&oe=utf-8&aq=t&channel=rcs

http://www.kcm.org/real-help/faith/speak/faith-confessions

chrome-extension://oemmndcbldboiebfnladdacbdfmadadm/https://www.billwinston.org/uploadedFiles/Faith%20Confession.pdf

http://biblehub.com/matthew/4-4.htm

http://www.biblemeanings.info/Words/Animal/Fishes.htm

http://www.patheos.com/blogs/christiancrier/2015/07/17/what-does-water-represent-in-the-bible-a-christian-study/

https://www.biblegateway.com/passage/?search=2+Corinthians+5%3A7&version=NKJV

chrome://bookmarks/

https://mail.google.com/mail/mu/mp/619/#tl/priority/%5Esmartlabel_personal

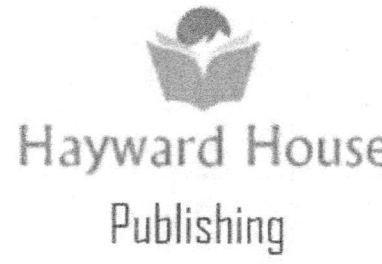

Hayward House

Publishing

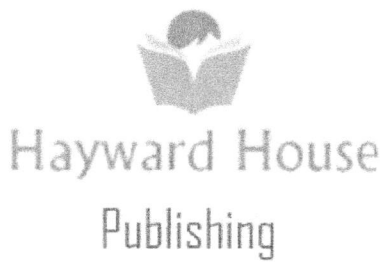

Hayward House
Publishing

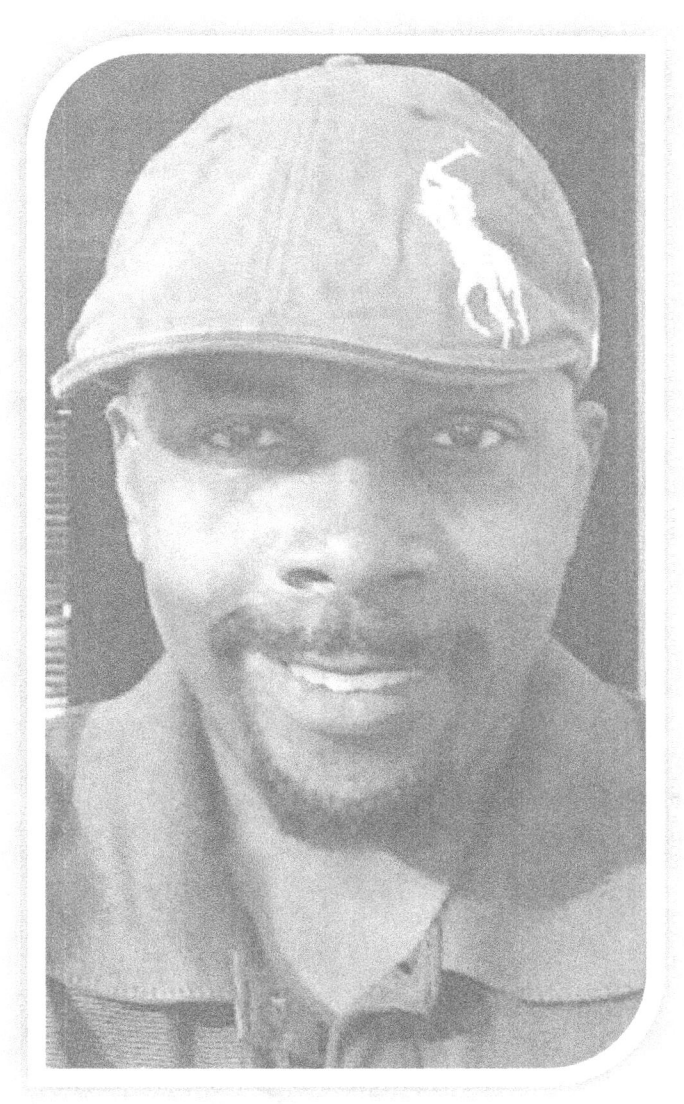

www.ingramcontent.com/pod-product-compliance
Lightning Source LLC
Chambersburg PA
CBHW081645220526
45468CB00009B/2557